# *Die Not Today*

A story of inspiration and hope

By Mary Louise Sanders

# Table of Contents

"All it takes is a beautiful smile

to hide an injured soul and

they will never notice how broken you really are."

Robin Williams

# Dedication

This book is dedicated to anyone who is struggling with the overwhelming stress that life throws at you and the desire to keep some sense of sanity and joy without becoming bitter.

Just a note:
I wasn't planning to write a book. I was in such a rage from things that had happened at work that I came home and started typing. What happened wasn't fair and the unfairness had been going on for over two years. I was saturated with frustration, anger, resentment and the feeling that I don't matter. First, I began typing details that occurred at work. When I was done, I was still so overwhelmed with anger that I began typing about things that occurred throughout my life. After a couple of days of venting about everything, I thought to myself, I can't be the only one going through this so I started organizing my life experiences into a book.

“Everyone you meet is fighting a battle

you know nothing about.

BE KIND ALWAYS”

Robin Williams

# Preface

- Have things gotten so bad that you can't take it anymore?
- Have you ever felt like you can't see the light at the end of the tunnel and feel like things won't get any better?
- Have you ever felt like you don't matter?

When I was four years old, my brother and sister were in school. From a four year olds perspective, I felt unwanted and unloved so I was sad most of the time and I refused to eat. I was very lonely. Mom did not want a third child and she let me know it ever since I was a little girl. When mom needed her space, which was almost every day, she would send me outside to play alone. One day, I was playing outside in the grass, barefoot, and I stepped on a bumble bee. I started crying loudly for mom. Mom yelled at me to come inside. I remember trying and saying, "I can't." In a rage, mom came outside, grabbed me by the arm, dragged me through the grass, up the cement walkway, up the cement stairs, through the house then sat me down on the back stair at the back of the house. She angrily ordered me to keep quiet. I sat there alone and quiet until my sister came home from school. Mom forced her to sit with me.

A year later, when I was old enough to go to kindergarten, I was afraid I would never be allowed to come back home. My sister had to walk me to school and sit with me before she could go to her class. During recess I would climb up the monkey bars and refuse to come down until my mother

“I used to think that the worst thing in life

was to end up alone.

It’s not.

The worst thing in life is to end up with people

who make you feel alone.”

Robin Williams

came and took me home.

As the years went by, I continued to feel alone and invisible to everyone in the house. I just didn't fit in.

I was constantly made to feel that there was something wrong with me and that I wasn't worth the time it took for them to smile at me or say "hello", "good morning", whatever, anything.

By the time I reached high school, I was suffering deep depression. One night, I put a very large bottle of aspirin on my nightstand. I was intending to take all of them, but first I asked God, "Give me one good reason why I shouldn't kill myself." I eventually went to sleep that night hoping I would get an answer.

When I woke up the next morning, I immediately heard a voice say,

*"Because you have not seen the beautiful world that I have created."*

His voice resounded in my mind. I realized I was too self involved in my little world and God let me know there is a big, beautiful world out there for me to see. All I needed to do was refocus my attention away from myself and be patient.

God spoke to me and I believe God speaks to anyone who believes in Him and who will listen. The best time to listen is when you are asleep, when your mind is at rest and not busy with day time thoughts, stresses and influences. People will

"Acknowledging the good

that you already have in your life

is the foundation for all abundance."

Eckhart Tolle

let you down, God won't.

You may think He doesn't love you or that He doesn't exist or that He doesn't care because He didn't give you what you want. *That is because we are spoiled.*

Scattered throughout the book, I mention all the different things I did to try to overcome my depression throughout the years.

Some worked, some didn't.  Just keep trying.

I am hoping that my journey in realizing the effect that God had on me throughout my life might influence those who gave up on God, or to those who don't believe or have doubts. If life isn't working without Him, then maybe life will work with Him.

A life with God allows us to see beyond ourselves.

A life with*out* God is hopelessness.

"Remember that sometimes

not getting what you want

is a wonderful stroke of luck."

Dalai Lama

1. David Was A Man After God's Heart

The story of David is what helped me deal with my guilt and I hope it helps those who are having a difficult time. I figured if God can forgive David for adultery and murder, then maybe God can forgive me for my sins and anyone else who feels the heavy burden of their actions. The problem was that I was unable to forgive myself.

It took years for me to figure out why some people were blessed who I didn't think deserved to be blessed. But fortunately for me, I realized that just because I don't like them, doesn't mean they don't deserve the blessings they received. God knows their heart. I don't. Just like God knows my heart, they don't.

So, what special characteristics did David have that God loved so much?

A. David did everything God asked him to do
Acts 13:22 NIV "After removing Saul, He made David their king. God testified concerning him: 'I found David, son of Jesse, a man after my own heart; *he will do everything I want him to do.*'"

B. David adored God's Law and meditated <u>daily</u> on His word. Psalm 119:47-48 NIV "For I delight in Your commands because I love them. I lift up my hands to your commands, which I love and I meditate on your decrees." God was a constant in David's life. The more you focus on God the less you sin and God loves it when you think of Him.

"But the Lord does not look at the things people look at. People look at the outward appearance, but the Lord looks at the heart."

1 Samuel 16:7

C. David was grateful and thankful when life was good but also when his life was threatened. To show God how grateful and thankful he was, he wrote most of the Psalms in the Bible.

D. David does *not* blame anyone for his errors and makes no attempt to excuse his actions. He takes full responsibility. 2 Samuel 11:2-5 describes David's sin with Bathsheba. David married the widowed Bathsheba, but their first child died as punishment from God for David's adultery and murder of Uriah. David repented his sins and Bathsheba later gave birth to Solomon. The words in Psalm 51:1-11 display absolute humility and anguish over his sin.

Psalm 51:1-11 NIV *Shortened* David's prayer for remorse.

"Have mercy on me, O God, according to your unfailing love; according to your great compassion, blot out my transgressions. Wash away all my iniquity and cleanse me from my sin. For I know my transgressions, and my sin is always before me. Against you, you only, have I sinned and done what is evil in your sight, create in me a pure heart, O God, and renew a steadfast spirit within me. Do not cast me from your presence or take your Holy Spirit from me."

People are always trying to steer you away from God and to follow them.

"To be *yourself* in a world

that is constantly trying to make you something else

is the greatest accomplishment."

Ralph Waldo Emerson

E. The Lord was David's shepherd to guide him every day.

Psalm 23 NIV David prayed: "The Lord is my shepherd, I shall not be in want. He makes me lie down in green pastures, He leads me beside quiet waters, He restores my soul. He guides me in paths of righteousness for His name's sake. Even though I walk through the valley of the shadow of death, I will fear no evil, for You are with me; Your rod and Your staff, they comfort me. You prepare a table before me in the presence of my enemies. You anoint my head with oil; my cup overflows. Surely goodness and love will follow me all the days of my life, and I will dwell in the house of the Lord forever."

Psalm 119:2-3 NIV "Blessed are those who keep His statutes and seek Him with *all* their heart. They do no wrong but follow His ways."

"You shall love the Lord your God

with all your heart

and with all your soul

and with all your mind."

Matthew 22:37

## 2. Can I Sin All I Want and Still Go To Heaven?

No! Blasphemy is not forgiven. But, maybe……if….

Blasphemy is the crime of *insulting, showing contempt* or *lack of respect* for God. For example, stealing over and over again is blasphemy. It is insulting, showing contempt and shows absolutely no respect for God and His laws.

It's as if you are giving God the middle finger.

The good news is if you make a mistake, feel remorse, ask God for forgiveness, repent, try not to do it again and take full responsibility, He will forgive you. The Ten Commandments was written long ago in an attempt to teach people how to treat one another. Respect God, respect your Parents (even if you don't like them or agree with them), don't steal, don't lie, don't covet, don't murder, don't commit adultery, remember the Sabbath and keep it holy, no idols (and that includes idolizing and coveting money), love only God and never use His name in vain are examples of the Ten Commandments.

How would you feel if someone stole from you? So don't you steal. If you don't want to be lied to, then don't lie. If you don't want anyone interfering with your marriage, then don't you interfere. Coveting other lifestyles to the point where you don't appreciate your own is very sad and destructive. There is no need to compare what you have with others.

"You have succeeded in life

when all you really want

is only

what you really need"

Vernon Howard

I am going to talk about Thou shalt not steal because working in retail I see a lot of it. One day at work, a man was headed towards the exit door pushing his cart filled with stuff. I said, "Excuse me sir, the cash registers are in that direction." He opened up his jacket so I could see his gun and said, "Are you going to make me?" I stepped aside speechless and let him pass. Whether or not he needed the stuff in his cart doesn't matter. Stealing is wrong.

It would be much safer for the employees if the company would hire police officers. I am sure that it costs less to hire police officers than the dollar amount of merchandise that is stolen every day.

Another incident was when a female walked into the store with nothing. She grabbed a cart and proceeded to fill it up. She walked over to customer service claiming she wanted to return everything. When the manager told her that she had to have a receipt, she took mace out of her purse and sprayed the manager in the eyes. Then she pushed the cart outside and put everything in her car.

The same people steal every week, over and over again. That is blasphemy and this is where I point out that you can not sin all you want and still go to heaven.

Every day I go to work not knowing what will happen next. The law protects those who are violent and steal and the employees are at their mercy.

Luke 23:34 "Father, forgive them for they know NOT what they do." The key word here is "NOT".

“No one can serve two masters.

Either he will hate the one and love the other,

or he will be devoted to the one and despise the other.

You cannot serve both God and money.”

Matthew 6:24-26

Jesus is <u>not</u> asking God to forgive those who <u>know</u> what they are doing.

TV personalities preach hope to people *which is nice,* but it is a shame they don't integrate into the hope the Ten Commandments and that bad behavior must stop and never be repeated.

Six years ago at work, this girl was sitting on the floor rocking back and forth praying, "God I need a Mustang". She repeated this one line over and over again for fifteen minutes. I waited for her to finish her prayer before I asked her what she was doing. She said, "Joel Osteen said to pray every day for something that you want and God will eventually give it to you."

I have yet to find a single prayer in the Bible that involves asking God for materialistic things. The prayers I have read in the Bible ask for forgiveness, strength, safety, etc. Even David did not ask God to save his son. Instead, David asked for mercy and forgiveness.

I may have missed a prayer or two because the Bible is immense, but God is more about intrinsic things. Intrinsic qualities come from within. For example, an intrinsic quality of a dog is that they're loyal. Doing a job because you love it is intrinsic because the motivation comes from within and is not because of money. It is understandable that a person take a job because it pays a lot and has good benefits, but if the job is ruining the quality of your life, it would be wise to save as much as you can so you can move on to do something you enjoy.

"Two things define you:

your patience when you have nothing and

your attitude when you have everything."

George Bernard Shaw.

When people come to you for guidance, give them hope so they can become great also. Maybe work with them on a course of action to help them repent, feel remorse and ask for a contrite heart instead of a car. Help them develop a renewed spirit so they can have a productive life. My car is old with over 106,000 miles on it and the dash is lit up like a Christmas tree but I can't afford to fix it. There are more constructive ways to earn money to pay the bills but it takes patience. I worked two jobs during Christmas when I was 68 years old and agreed with family and friends not to spend money on gifts. That in itself saved a lot of money and reduced a lot of stress and to be honest, I had the happiest Christmas I have ever had.

Realize you are not a good role model for your family (children) or friends or strangers that watch you steal.

"Each person must live their life as a model for others." Rosa Parks

Matthew 26:27-28 NIV "Drink from it, all of you. This is my 'blood of the covenant', which is poured out for *many* for the forgiveness of sins." The key word in all of this is the word *"many"*, NOT *"all"*.

“Great people

are those who make others feel

that they too can become great.”

Mark Twain

Not everyone will be forgiven.

Matthew 20:28, Mark 10:45: NIV "Just as the Son of Man did not come to be served, but to serve, and to give his life as a ransom for *many*." Again, the key word here is "many" NOT "everyone."

Not everyone can be saved.

People go to church, ask for forgiveness, then walk out the door and continue their bad behavior. Somewhere a line needs to be drawn. I believe Jesus gives unconditional love but disobedience and repetition of committing the same sin will NOT be blessed.

Moses never made it to the promised land. Think about it.

Think about this also, Jesus told His disciples to leave everything behind. This is because Jesus was not about materialistic stuff.

Matthew 12:31 NIV "And so I tell you, every kind of sin and slander can be forgiven, but blasphemy against the Spirit will not be forgiven. It states the same in Mark 3:28-29 NIV and also in Luke 10 NIV

Hebrews 6:6 NIV
".... To their loss they are crucifying the Son of God all over again and subjecting him to public disgrace."

“Smart people learn from everything and everyone,

average people from their experiences,

stupid people

already have all the answers.”

Socrates

3. Mercy

Matthew 5:7-9
"Blessed are the merciful, for they will be shown mercy.
Blessed are the pure in heart, for they will see God.
Blessed are the peacemakers, for they will be called sons of God."

Mercy isn't something that is practiced daily by most people. There are so many people (including Christians) who are overly opinionated. They say things that cut straight to the heart.

Jesus never said an unkind word to anyone. He spoke to Mary Magdalene when no one else would and befriended her and because of His kindness, she changed into a better person.

Why can't we show kindness when someone does something we believe is a sin? Why do we feel we have to judge everyone but ourselves? When we act out violently toward the sinner, that is just as much a sin as the person we are angry toward.

For example, how many people condemn those who get an abortion and sometimes resort to violence and/or murder? The girl getting the abortion is already stressed out and maybe even hysterical, or, what about the girl who was raped? And what about the girl and/or boy who was sexually, physically or emotionally abused for years as a child? What about the foster child bouncing from home to home never feeling loved enough to keep. Maybe they are trying to spare

“The world is changed by your example,

not

by your opinion”

Paulo Coelho

that child from the hell they lived through.

God knows the hearts of all people, *let Him deal with each one* according to all they do. John 8:7 "He who is without sin, cast the first stone". Everyone is guilty of sin. Everyone. Stop taking matters into your own hands. If anything, educate.

My dad told me not to judge anyone without walking a mile in their shoes. How can you walk a mile in their shoes if you have never experienced what they went through? This is where mercy comes in. You may not understand what that person is going through because you have never been through it, but show mercy anyway. God knows their heart and He knows your heart. If your heart cruelly judges someone, God will cruelly judge you.

Colossians 3:12-17
"Therefore, as God's chosen people, holy and dearly loved, clothe yourselves with compassion, kindness, humility, gentleness and patience. Bear with each other and forgive whatever grievances you may have against one another. Forgive as the Lord forgave you. And over all these virtues *put on love,* which binds them all together in perfect unity."

Keep your opinions to yourself and your mouth shut and let God work on their spirit. Instead of chastising them, pray for them that they find God and that they open their hearts so God can live there. Less mistakes are made when a person is treated with kindness. The same kindness Jesus showed Mary.

“It may be that the Lord will see my distress

and repay me with good

for the cursing I am receiving today.”

2 Samuel 16:12

## 4. Divorce

I am approaching this subject because there are a lot of people who ostracize a person for being divorced. I know this from personal experience. It creates a very lonely and hurtful environment and because of these people, a lot of good people turn away from God and church. Ministers receive an education from Seminary, but obviously some can't see the forest through the trees or else they would show compassion and say things to make people feel better and to give them hope, not guilt. You would be surprised at how many people commit suicide because of the guilt imposed on them from people who think they know everything. Trust me, they don't know everything.

Thou shalt not get divorced is NOT one of the Ten Commandments. I do not believe that all divorces result in adultery. And the concept of adultery has been defined and redefined many times throughout the ages by people not God. I believe that the message to be received from all of this is to not have sexual relations with a lot people. It creates a hard hearted person who no longer feels the emotional benefit of love.

Regardless, it is a forgivable sin. The advice I was given is if your first marriage fails, wait ten years before you marry again. During that time you can have fun and enjoy life, and hopefully learn what it is you <u>need</u>. Marriage isn't the fantasy a lot of people think it is and it is expensive and stressful, especially if you have children. And, It is possible that because divorcees are told they are going to go to hell, that they don't care anymore. Why should they? They are going to go to hell anyway, what do they have to lose?

John 8:2-9 NIV

2 At dawn He appeared again in the temple
courts, where all the people gathered around
Him, and He sat down to teach them. 3 The
teachers of the law and the Pharisees brought
in a woman caught in adultery. They made her
stand before the group 4 and said to Jesus,
"Teacher, this woman was caught in the act of
adultery. 5 In the Law, Moses commanded us to
stone such women. Now what do you say?" 6
They were using this question as a trap, in order
to have a basis for accusing Him. But Jesus
bent down and started to write on the ground
with His finger 7 When they kept on questioning
Him, He straightened up and said to them, "Let
any one of you who is without sin be the first to
throw a stone at her." 8 Again He stooped down
and wrote on the ground. 9 At this, those who
heard began to go away one at a time, the older
ones first, until only Jesus was left, with the
woman still standing there.

Jesus chose forgiveness instead of violence.

In the case of my divorce, if we had taken the time to get to know one another, we both would have agreed not to get married. We had nothing in common. I rushed in because my mother and I had our issues, the dream of getting married was exciting, getting out of the house was even more exciting, and my future husband was a very nice and responsible person. But, I was not mature enough to fully understand the accumulation of trauma that I had been through in my life and my husband had no idea of the baggage he was marrying.

He had bouts of violence which was caused by the frustration of being married to me. Because my husband was a good person, he realized with the help of his mother, the extent of what was happening and knew he had to stop. He deserves kudos for that and it was a blessing that our divorce was amicable. But, I fell out of love with him. Any kind of abuse acts like a light switch in my heart. I would rather be lonely. I just did not have the courage to divorce him because I knew my dad would be disappointed. I couldn't handle that. But, after my dad passed away, I asked for a divorce because life is short. I was only 25 years old and I could not imagine spending the next 50 years being miserable.

Because my dad told me never to get a divorce, I suffered depression and guilt. A friend took me to talk to a female minister hoping she could help. She told me that if I do not go back with my husband, I will be guilty of forcing him to commit adultery and I will go to hell. I told her that my God is a loving God and, if I was going to go to hell, I would have lots of company and proceeded to walk away.

“Knowing when to walk away is wisdom.

Being able to walk away is courage.

Walking away with your head held high is dignity.”

Unknown

Her words hung over me like a black cloud and I hated myself for years.

I did not have the understanding then that I have now. The Ten Commandments were revealed to Moses and inscribed by the finger of God and divorce is not mentioned. Moses created a certificate of divorce because men were hard hearted and if I understand it correctly, it was to protect the divorced wife so she was left with something to help her after her husband kicked her out.

Mark 10:1-5 "....Jesus went into the region of Judea and across the Jordan. Again crowds of people came to him, and as was his custom, he taught them. Some Pharisees came and tested him by asking, "Is it lawful for a man to divorce his wife?" "What did Moses command you?" He replied. They said, "Moses permitted a man to write a certificate of divorce and send her away." *"it was because your hearts were hard that Moses wrote you this law," Jesus replied.*

1 John 1:17 NIV For the law was given through Moses; grace and truth came through Jesus Christ.

From the time of Moses to the time of Jesus, adultery has resulted in death or going to hell. Thanks to Jesus, if we repent and never do it again, we are forgiven. God knows our heart and He will deal with us as He sees fit.

Matthew 5:28 "But I say to you that everyone who looks at a woman with lustful intent has already committed adultery with her in his heart."

“Experience is a hard teacher

because she gives the test first,

the lesson afterward”

Vernon Sanders Law

As long as you repent and try not to do it again, you are forgiven. Lust is a strong feeling and requires a tremendous amount of internal strength in order to stay away. In some cases, it is best to never be alone with the person you are lusting after so you won't be tempted.

Lust is often confused with love which is why it is important to take it slow. It takes a long time to get to know someone. Listen to the words that come out of their mouth because it represents the mindset of the person speaking them.

Time answers this question, "Are you in love with the person you are having fun with or are you in love with the fun? Did you finally find someone you enjoy being with then they end it? It leaves you numb and in shock. There is a chance you are missing the rituals of camaraderie and that is not the same as love.

The longer you wait to have sex with a person, the better you get to know them and that is crucial to a long lasting relationship. I dated this one guy for a year and later discovered he had many sexual relationships with many different women including girls in my high school. These are things you want to know before getting married and I thank God I found out in time to break up with him.

So no matter what decision you make, God knows what you are going through but He needs to know that you recognize the mistake and that you are sorry. Learning from it saves you heartache and pain.

It took me years to put it all together.

“Every adversity, every failure, every heartache

carries with it the seed

of an equal or greater benefit.”

Napoleon Hill

I was tired of feeling bad about myself for being divorced, so I stopped going to church. I met more hippocrates and self-righteous people in church, than people who do not go to church. I wasn't getting anything out of it except condemnation and a broken heart. It worked out for the best because I began spending more time with God on a daily basis and that has helped me a lot.

Divorce leaves a person with a sense of loss. Time will show that God has a better life ahead of you and you will be surprised that it is better than the one you lost.

There is only one sin that differs from the rest and that is blasphemy. It is not forgiven. So, divorce, adultery and all the other sins that we as humans commit, are forgiven if we are truly sorry. Everyone makes mistakes. The mistakes may differ, but the concept is the same. Mistakes cause sin and sin is sin. There is no reason to feel such extreme guilt that you would want to end your life or spend every day feeling miserable.

Because I took the time to write down all the good things that have happened in my life, I was able to realize that God has forgiven me. He would not have blessed me with so much if He hadn't. So, no matter what anyone says, I know I was forgiven even though people say otherwise. The same goes for you. So if you are depressed, please look outside the bubble you are in, observe everything that is good and beautiful and blind yourself to the people who have destructive things to say. Constructive criticism is good to hear even if it hurts, but destructive criticism can be debilitating if you listen to it.

"The pessimist sees difficulty

in every opportunity.

The optimist sees opportunity

in every difficulty."

Winston Churchill

It takes both rain and sunshine to make rainbows. That doesn't mean you have to drown in the rain. Divorce is not the end, it is the rainbow representing your new life.

"You must never be fearful about

what you are doing

when it is right."

Rosa Parks

## 5. Turning Point

It took years for me to realize the importance of the past events and God's role in it. I didn't realize that what happened next in my life would be the turning point that changed my life forever and for the better.

Back in 1977 - 78, My husband and I moved to Virginia. He was hired by George Mason University as a Programmer and I eventually got hired as a Secretary in the Sociology Department. I met a really nice African American teacher there who changed my life forever. We were talking one day and he told me he went to college on full scholarship because of his high GPA. I told him I couldn't get anything higher than a C and asked him how he got such high grades. He told me it was probably because no one taught me how to study. He told me to register for a class I am interested in and not to worry about whether it was a requirement. After I registered for a class and bought my book, I waited for him to walk by my desk to ask him to teach me how to study. I picked Psychology 101. I hoped the class would give me insight into my issues. He taught me how to study and I got an A. Ever since then I was a straight A student except when I took more than three classes, then I got a B.

My husband only needed about 30 hours to graduate, so we went to school together at University of Maryland University College for weekend and evening classes. I remember calling my dad up and telling him the good news about my GPA. Dad said that he was proud of me and that I had something more important than a high GPA. He said I had common sense and wisdom and that I was smarter than my

"I will do what you have asked, moreover,

I will give you what you have not asked for."

1 Kings 3:12-13

sister and brother put together. That was the first time in my life my father said he was proud of me. I waited *twenty-five* years to hear one complement and it felt good.

Sadly, shortly after our phone call, my dad passed away on May 7, 1979 at 64 years of age. Soon after his death, I asked my husband to leave. I was saturated by people who made me feel bad about myself and when I told my husband I wanted to be a programmer like him, he smirked and told me I wasn't smart enough. Well, that was it. I was done feeling like a stupid loser. Twenty-five years was long enough. He had a place to go live and I didn't. He was very kind and he temporarily moved in with his mother. I loved my mother-in-law more than I loved my own mother. I felt loved by her and she made me feel like I was an important member of the family. She taught me how to crochet and make all sorts of crafts. I loved her so much. My husband was kind enough to pay the rent for one year after we split until our divorce went through.

After graduating from UMUC, which took me years, I went to Computer Learning Center in Springfield, Virginia for six months to learn programming. I wasn't the best but I did okay. Shortly after finishing CLC, I got hired thanks to the recommendation from a wonderful person. It was a challenge but it felt good to get a job in something that I was told that I was not smart enough to do.

One day, I made a flow chart from one of the programs that was already written and pointed out that the numbers were truncating because the field wasn't large enough. I was told that I did a good job.

“The most difficult thing is the decision to act,

The rest is merely tenacity.”

Amelia Earhart

But, I felt that I wasn't as good as I would have liked and I was tired of working in an office. I wanted a job that helped me enjoy life more so I started looking for another job in both the Washington Star and the Washington Post. One day, I had a conversation with my manager. He gently told me things I needed to hear about my attitude. It was difficult to hear but I appreciated his kindness.

Anyway, I found another job. It was a temporary six month position teaching military personnel how to use their brand new computer system. We were given the status of Lt. Colonel. We traveled to military hospitals in groups of two and in November I was sent to Wiesbaden Germany. During Thanksgiving, I hooked up with a girl who was teaching in Frankfort and her boyfriend and traveled through different parts of Germany.

I can not begin to describe my feeling of happiness. I was away from my toxic family and in a place where I was regarded with respect. It felt so good and I savored every moment.

Anyway, I kind of nagged her to go to the Zugspitze. She agreed and we took a cable car to the top. I tried skiing and found myself skiing down the summit on my bottom. I laughed all the way down the hill with a smile on my face that would not go away.

After I got back up the summit, I went into the building that had food and souvenirs. My friend and her boyfriend kept on skiing. I bought a souvenir then went outside and stood alone looking at the majestic mountains, the sky, the clouds,

"Let your speech always be gracious,

seasoned with salt,

so that you may know how

you should answer each person."

Colossians 4:6

the cross, the snow, and watched skiers ski down the summit.

I just stood there in awe, staring at the beautiful scenery without a single thought going through my mind when a voice resounded in my head,

*"This is what I meant when I told you that you haven't seen the beautiful world that I have created."*

I couldn't move.

I felt a wave of warmth and love go through my body like I have never felt before. I felt God's forgiveness for all of my sins. I stood there until it was time to go, embracing every second of every minute.

The journey to the Zugspitze closed the full circle in my life from when I was in high school thinking about not waking up the next day to standing in awe of immense beauty hearing God's voice reminding me of the beautiful world that He created.

“To live is the rarest thing in the world.

Most people exist,

that is all.”

Oscar Wilde

## 6. After The Turning Point In My Life

After reaching a full circle in my life, what next? Another full circle to accomplish? My six month position was over and I had a mortgage and no job. I had a savings account, but that was running low. I dropped my pride and met mom for lunch and asked for $1,000 so I could make my mortgage payment. I had never asked my mother for anything ever. She said she couldn't because my brother and sister had tapped her out. She didn't have anything left to give. Crazy as this sounds, I understood.

God stepped in and Bob, the person who sold me my house, helped me get a job at Bendix in the computer room at NASA in Greenbelt, Maryland. I think I was told that I would not have gotten the job if it wasn't for Bob's referral.

I loved my job in the computer room. I was treated with respect. It was a "feel good about yourself" kind of job. One day, I noticed a computer programmer had walked into the computer room and looked at the top page of four reports then left. Each report printed was at least 1-2 inches of paper. The next day I asked him why he only looked at the first page of each report. He said that he only looked at the report if it had an error. So I asked him, "why not insert an 'if' statement so it will print only if there is an error? Why waste all that paper"? He was nice and said, "Why didn't I think of that?" He also went so far as to give me the paperwork to fill out for an award for saving the government money. How honest is that?

“In the middle of difficulty lies opportunity.

Albert Einstein

Life was going well. Then one day I went to the break room where there was a cute security guard sitting at his post. Security guards move around a lot. We started talking and he seemed like he was a nice person. But, several months later, before we started dating, I saw him outside one of the buildings at NASA screaming, cursing and making a scene. His friend/coworker tried to calm him down. What was I thinking when I started dating him? I wasn't.

Next time I saw him, he told me he was hoping that I didn't see the scene he had made. He told me he was embarrassed and that he wanted to ask me out. We started dating. I rationalized at the time it was a one time thing. The future would reveal how wrong I was.

Meanwhile, one day I was told there was a vacancy on the COBE project. I applied for the job and asked my manager, Mr. Rice, if I could transfer. He agreed and I got the position. I was so excited. There were two positions in the MOR at COBE: Sr Ops Controller and Ops Controller. It is like the difference between a pilot and co-pilot. My position was obviously co-pilot. After a couple of months, I took the certification test and passed.

I loved my job! Everything in my life was going well.

On cold, icy wintery nights, the security guard I was dating would warm up my car and scrape the ice off the windshield just before it was time for me to get off work. Even when it was his day off, he would drive to work and warm up my car. On my birthday he bought me a bicycle. He had a friend help him transport it because it would not fit in his Z28.

Never blame anyone in your life.

Bad people give you experience.

Worst people give you a lesson.

Good people give you happiness.

The best people give you memories.

Unknown

I look back and I am ashamed at how rude I was. I didn't want a girls bike. I wanted to ride a boys bike. But he never complained. He and his friend went out and exchanged it.

Why did I want a boy's bike? Because I had a gut feeling that I was going to eventually have a baby boy and I wanted my future son to have it. Guess what? Years later, I had a boy and we still have the bicycle! William rode it until he outgrew it. Funny how things fall into place if you notice.

But, things started to spiral out of control. I became overwhelmed. My mind was consumed with stress and I wasn't focused on God on a daily basis like I used to. I made the mistake of lending him $1500 to refinance his Z28. He was supposed to pay me back $100 a month.

Next thing I know, he was pushing me into helping him buy a truck. He said he hated his job and wanted to start a landscaping business. He found one but needed another $1500 as a down payment. I told him no at first. I told him not until he paid me back. He put the pressure on and told me he would pay me back with the money he earned landscaping. When he wanted something, he was like a little kid nagging me until I gave in. What was I thinking? I obviously wasn't. I helped him buy the truck. Then he said he wouldn't have to pay me back if I married him. Hah!!! Not happening. There was no way I was going to marry him.

It had been a year since we started dating and I was ready to end it.

I tried and he cried.

“I believe that everything happens for a reason.

People change so that you can learn to let go,

things go wrong so that you appreciate them

when they’re right,

you believe lies so you eventually learn to trust

no one but yourself,

and sometimes good things fall apart

so better things can fall together.”

Marilyn Monroe

Out of frustration, he shoved me against the wall and I hit my head. Next thing I knew I was in his truck and he was driving me down to the courthouse. All the way over I was unable to speak.

When we were in the room with the Justice of the Peace, I refused to say, "I do." But, after a moment of silence I said, "I do" but I refused to sign his last name in the register. He noticed. I couldn't stop thinking about how I was going to get out of this.

Then one day, he mentioned that his name was not on the mortgage. I told him it never will. I was riding my bicycle in the exercise room, when I heard God's voice in my head say, *"He is going to ruin you."* I should have gone to see a counselor of some kind but I have a tendency to crawl inside myself when things get really bad instead of seeking help. If I only knew then what I know now.

We had fun spending our days off looking at houses. I had no intention of getting a new house because I knew in my heart he was going to ruin me.

Unfortunately, I got caught up in his orbit and we found a house that I loved and it was marked down $20,000 for a quick sale. I couldn't pass on the equity.

So what happened?

"Stand for something or you will

fall for anything.

Today's mighty oak is yesterday's nut

that held it's ground."

Rosa Parks

All I know is that I loved my job and he hated his. I helped him find another job hoping that would resolve his anger issues. After his first day at his new job, he came home, slammed the door, and yelled, “Everyone is an $%#@*” I stood there in shock. The person who used to be so nice to me turned into a monster. The same monster I saw outside the building at NASA before we started dating.

I thought the job was causing him to be angry, but that anger stems from issues that occurred long before he even met me. God warned Me! He showed me his temper before we started dating.

"The greatest glory in living

lies not in never falling,

but rising every time we fall."

Nelson Mandela

## 7. Leaving Everything Behind

The disciples left everything to follow Jesus and until it happened to me I didn't realize what a difficult and stressful transition it had to be for them. That took a lot of faith. I left almost everything behind to move to Kentucky. I had rented a house prior to my move so I had the security of knowing we had a roof over our heads. But the disciples didn't have that security. They lived day to day not really knowing what was going to happen next. Their faith in Jesus was greater than their fear of the unknown.

I was overwhelmed with stress and it was traumatizing because I didn't want to leave Maryland. I tried to talk to my husband so I could stay. I called once a week for six weeks to try and negotiate custody, visitation and the house. The phone calls always left me despondent. I always called right before my weekly appointment with my psychologist so we could talk about it.

Every week it was the same. He gets the child, he gets the house, I can not visit because I am unfit, I have to pay him alimony, child support and the mortgage while he lives in the house with our son. The house was supposed to be mine in the event of a divorce because I put $50,000 down on the house and I paid every single mortgage payment. He obviously went back on his word. He sabotaged every effort I made to stay in Maryland and keep my job and my home and our son.

“Success is not final, failure is not fatal:

It is the courage to continue that counts.”

Winston Churchill

I know my husband did not listen to the words that came out of his mouth because if he did, he would have realized the threats and potential violence he was proposing. He would have realized that he gave me no choice but to leave Maryland to protect our son. His inability to calm down and work things out so I could live in my home and stay at my job resulted in the house going into foreclosure. Basically, he was leaving my son and I homeless.

Except for furniture, clothing and my car, I left everything behind that I loved and moved to Kentucky with my ten day old child. I couldn't have done it without the help and support from my mother, Charles Houchins and Bob Simmons. I was so traumatized I couldn't stop crying. In the beginning after I moved in with my mother, I started working on a counted cross-stitch of Jesus.

Every stitch I said a prayer. A short one. Some prayers were for me, some were for Steve (even though I hated him) and some were for my son. When I prayed for Steve, I was filled with so much hate that I tried hard not to wish that he would drown, or get run over by a bus, or fall into a deep ravine, or get consumed with fire, or.......use your own imagination!!!

I cried a lot. I desperately needed everything to be okay, especially for my son. It took ten months to finish the cross-stitch of Jesus and to feel a modicum of peace. Cross-stitching and praying with every stitch helped but very, very slowly. I am ashamed that I wished such terrible thoughts on my husband. I guess that is what rage does to a person.

"Anger is an acid that can do more harm

to the vessel in which it is stored

than to anything on which it is poured."

Mark Twain

I am sorry to say, living with mom was hell. There were good days, but the bad days were so bad that it resulted in forgetting the good days. One Easter morning, mom came downstairs dressed and ready to go to church. William was approximately 18-months old. When she saw that William and I were still in our pajamas, she went into a rage. She started screaming at me, "You better get dressed and get in the car." I just stood there in shock. Then mom leaned towards Williams' face and screamed at him, "You Don't Love Me because if you did, you would go to church with me." William started crying, "I do love you Nana, I do love you." Mom got madder and kept screaming, "No you don't. No you don't.

I finally got out of my trance and *screamed*, "GO. Don't yell at my son. GO. Get out." I picked William up and held him close. He was crying and I was crying. When William calmed down, I put in a Barney tape. I called Charles Houchins and told him I didn't want to live anymore. I felt trapped. No job and no home of my own.

He immediately drove to Kentucky to bring me back to Maryland. I followed in my car. A friend named Christine allowed me to stay in her home while she went on vacation. At the end of I think 10 days, I followed Charles back to Kentucky. I <u>wish</u> I had asked Charles if I could move in with him and try to get my job back at NASA. I was an Ops Controller and Mission Planner working on the GRO project for Bendix at that time. I loved my job and was heartbroken when my husband saw to it that I left Maryland. I also knew Charles was the nicest person in the world and I wish we could have stayed friends. But, he eventually got married and

“You define your own life.

Don’t let other people write your script.”

Oprah Winfrey

did the right thing by his wife. If more husbands and wives had this attitude, there would be fewer people committing adultery.

To help my depression and helplessness, I took very long walks every day pushing my son in a stroller. Some walks were three hours long. It was good for my son also. He enjoyed seeing the beauty that surrounded him, totally clueless to the horror that was going on in my life. The trees and the eventual changing colors of the leaves; the wildlife; other people walking or running; all the different dogs on leashes and everything wonderful that was going on around him. I would not have been able to enjoy being with my son full-time if it was not for my mother. She gets kudos for that. I tried almost every day to make her happy as my way of giving thanks. I stripped the wallpaper and painted every room in the house as per her request and I did all of her yard work.

So, why would I take care of my mother after decades of neglect and abuse, both verbal and physical?

I think I did it because I watched my father do it. When I was in high school, I asked my father why he wouldn't divorce my mother. She was very cruel and hard-hearted towards him. He said that there would be two sets of expenses and not enough money to send us to college. He also told me he wanted to come home from work everyday and see his children. Knowing they were safe and healthy meant more to him than his freedom.

“Nothing is impossible.

The word itself says,

I’m possible

Audrey Hepburn

He once told me never to marry so I wouldn't face the trauma of divorce if it didn't work out.

If only I had listened!!

So, I guess I got my sense of responsibility from him. I think I survived in Kentucky because I avoided mom as often as I could. I started working when William was three and a half years old. I saved all my money and was able to buy a condo so William and I could live a life in peace. It also gave mom space from me. I made sure that at least 5 days a week she could see her grandson but it was important that every night we went home to our condo. Even though I did not need mom's name on the loan, I put it there so mom could have the tax write off. It was my way of thanking her for putting up with me for six years.

Thank you God for being my rock and helping me through everything. I could not have done it without You.

"The two most powerful warriors

are patience and time"

Leo Tolstoy

8. Does God give us more than we can handle?

I have been told my entire life that God does not give us more than we can handle. All I can say is that God must think highly of my internal strength. Phew. I have been put through the wringer so many times I couldn't even count and what is totally annoying is that most of it was my own fault.

I decided to google this question and this is what I found.

In 1 Corinthians 10:13 (NIV) Paul does say, "God will not let you be tempted beyond what you can bear."

So, the truth is that God never said he would not give us more than we can handle.

A good example is the story of Job. Satan challenged God stating that Job was faithful <u>only</u> because he had everything he wanted. So God took everything away from Job to prove Satan wrong. This story showed that devotion to God with unrelenting loyalty, tenacity and patience no matter how bad things got is rewarding. It also shows how manipulative and destructive Satan is and that we should never listen to him.

Job 42:10: "<u>After Job had prayed for his friends</u>, the Lord restored his fortunes and gave him twice as much as he had before.

While Job suffered, he never stole anything to ease his burden. He only prayed for forgiveness and mercy.

So, where does that take us from here? How do we conquer overwhelming events?

"There is nothing impossible

to those who will try."

Alexander the Great

Keeping God a constant in our lives and patience, I believe, is first because it takes time to fix things in your life. Sometimes, it can take years. It took me years to graduate from college so I could earn a better income. I paid as I went along so I would not have the burden of debt.

Noticing and appreciating the little things that God does to help us feel better, I believe, is second. Sometimes we don't notice them because they are small, tender moments that happen quickly and our minds are consumed with larger problems. If the littlest things can make you happy, then you will experience more joy in your life.

When I was in high school, a friend told me about a little boy who was dying of a brain tumor. The little boy told his sister that if she really wants to be happy, truly happy, that she needs to notice the tiniest things in life, like one blade of grass and the chatter of the early morning birds.

That story touched my heart so much that when I was walking home from school that day, I decided to observe and listen to the littlest things. It is true. I went from being sad most of the time to being more joyful.

God coordinates small tender loving moments everyday for all of us, if we would only notice.

God is good. He is always there and He cares.

I am thankful for the little things that He does.

He gives us hope!

"Don't judge each day by the harvest you reap

but by the seeds that you plant."

Robert Louis Stevenson

## 9. What Did You Just Say?

David was God's favorite and he is my favorite also because he doesn't blame anyone for anything. He holds himself accountable. The people I have met in my life: family, friends, and coworkers rarely do. When I was young, my brother threw me onto the hard basement floor. He never showed remorse. I hit my head hard and his friend Dean said loudly, "You shouldn't have done that!!!" Dean stood there frozen while I layed on the floor. My brother said, "Sit down, we are missing Combat." But Dean didn't move until I slowly stood up." I remember holding my head because it hurt so much. I went upstairs and my mother and father were sitting on the sofa. They didn't even take me to the hospital. They told me to go to my room and stay there. My brother never apologized and mom and dad never made him apologize. He wasn't even punished. I felt worthless.

Very few people listen to the words that come out of their mouth, so they don't realize exactly how hurtful they are.

And because the words they say are at the spur of the moment, they often forget that they said it.

But, the person hearing their words never forgets.

My mother held a grudge against dad until the day ***she*** died in 2017 (45 years after dad died!). Whatever happened occurred before I was born in 1954 which makes it over 60-years of anger, bitterness, rage and grudges. She was hard-hearted towards my dad and provoked him alot. It is a blessing he was not a violent man.

“Holding on to anger is like grasping a hot

coal with the intent of throwing it at someone else;

You are the one who gets burned.”

Buddha

One day, maybe two to three months before mom died, I went to get her out of bed. She was in a terrible, hateful mood so she must have had a terrible dream. I lifted her into her wheelchair and took her to the bathroom, helped her shower, wash her hair, put clean clothes on her, lifted her into her wheelchair then took her to the living room to watch tv. After I lifted her into her electric recliner, I started toward the kitchen to fix her breakfast when I heard the whirring of the electric motor. I stopped and turned to see what was happening because mom would sometimes forget she couldn't walk. Mom slowly turned her head towards me. (reminded me of the Exorcist) She had this distorted, angry look on her face and said, "Yoouuurrr father didn't love you. He wanted me to have an abortion."

I said, "What did you just say?"

When mom had to think about what she said in order to repeat it, her eyes grew very large, her mouth dropped open, she clasped her hands together and bowed her head down. I went into the kitchen and made her favorite homemade banana blueberry pancakes from scratch. When I returned with her food, mom looked up at me and said, "I guess I am not as nice as I thought I was."

I said, "No mom, you are not. You've been telling me that since I was a little girl."

Mom angrily said, "*I have not*."

I said, "That's because you don't listen to the words that come out of your mouth."

“Be the change you wish to

see in the world.”

Gandhi

I wanted mom to know that I talked to dad about it in high school. So I told her that he told me that he was playing the devil's advocate. He said she was impossible to live with after she found out she was pregnant with their third child and every day was a living hell. I told her that he told me that he tried to reenlist in the army and be sent to another country so he could get some peace. Mom lowered her head and started eating.

Mom did not want a third child and obviously she did not get her way. Every time she looked at me she was reminded of a child she didn't want.

She didn't realize that I was a gift from God because God knew that my brother and sister would not be there to take care of her. So, He gave her a gift. Me. Someone to take care of her in her old age and not stick her in a nursing home.

Mom was always there for my brother and sister. But God knew they would not be there for her. I suffered sleep deprivation for years. One morning, around 2am on February 2, 2017, I went to bed thinking she finally fell asleep. Three hours later I woke up from her loud breathing. I tried to wake her up. EMTs came and took her to the hospital. The MRI showed that she had a massive stroke and was never to recover. So, in the hospital, my son on one side of the bed and I on the other side, held her hand while they removed life support. We stayed there until they said it was over.

“The only true wisdom is in knowing

we know nothing.”

Socrates

## 10. Loneliness, Emptiness, Hurt, Frustration, Anger

Loneliness makes a person feel unwanted and empty inside. Through the years, I had asked my brother and sister for help. My brother had an excuse for a while. His wife woke up one day paralyzed. But one day a few years later, I asked my brother if he and his wife would fly over so I can get some sleep. He told me no because his wife was still very sick and could not fly. I got on Facebook shortly after his rejection to discover that he and his wife flew to West Virginia to visit their son and daughter-in-law before they moved to Pennsylvania. West Virginia is a short flight to Kentucky and my mother would have paid for the flight. I saw the pictures of my brother, his wife, their son, daughter-in-law, and their baby. Considering the history of my relationship with my brother I shouldn't have been surprised. My brother eventually texted me that I could have his third of the inheritance for taking care of mom.

My sister did not have an excuse except that she was an angry and bitter person just like mom. My sister and her two children moved in with mom when one son was two years old and the other son was four years old. Mom allowed them to live with her until they left for college. My sister was never grateful for the sacrifices mom made so she and her children could live there. So, when I asked if she would fly over (from California) to help me out, I was not surprised when she told me, "no" and suggested putting her in a nursing home. She told me I could have her third of the inheritance if I would never ask her again.

Loneliness is not being alone,

It is the feeling that no one cares."

Unknown

Ten months after mom died, my brother and sister hired an attorney to sue me for their third of the estate!!!!

I was in such a rage I thought I was having a heart attack. I layed on the sofa clutching my chest, unable to breathe. My body felt like I was being stabbed by a thousand pins. It took half an hour to calm down. I layed on the sofa and prayed and turned on a tv show to take my mind off of what was happening.

I didn't contest it. It would not have done me any good and it was out of my control. God can deal with them.

I needed the money for the years I was unable to work while they were able to work. I have to work now because mom left me with more debt than I can afford.

What's ironic is that I could have sued my brother who was executor of our dad's estate back in 1979. One day, I was home in my apartment in Virginia, my husband was at work, and a voice told me to get to mom's house quickly. The house was a split-level type home. When I got there, mom was in the kitchen. She looked up and when she saw me standing in the doorway, she put her head down and scrubbed the counter top harder. She never said hello. My brother and sister were in the living room laying claim to dad's personal belongings. They couldn't see me until I walked up the stairs. My brother said to my sister, *"I forgot about her."* My sister gave me a camera and a book but my brother didn't give me anything. So, my brother did not fulfill his duties as executor fairly.

"Live as if you were to die tomorrow.

Learn as if you were to live forever.

An eye for an eye will only make the whole world blind."

Gandhi

Needless to say, I went through another period of frustration, hurt and anger and malevolence. I do believe in karma, so every time I would wish harm to them I would pray for forgiveness. It wasn't easy but prayer worked which freed me up to take control of my life and get my spiritual power back.

So now, years later, if anyone says "I don't care" or does something to show they don't care, or that I am worthless, it is a trigger that brings back terrible feelings.

Why can't people let go? I think it is because they never get closure.

I will never get closure for the years of abuse from my mother, sister or brother. The only reason I have peace is because they are far away and I don't have to ever see or talk to them again.

Only through God, His son, reading Bible verses; watching comedies and murder mysteries; reading books and articles that are positive; doing crafts like knitting, crocheting or needle work, working on this book and <u>exercise</u> can I find peace. Taking walks has helped me a lot. And when no one is around, I sing. I don't know the words to any songs but I sing gibberish (scat) like Ella Fitzgerald. It's fun.

“Our greatest ability as humans is

not to change the world,

but to change ourselves.”

Gandhi

## 11. Conclusion

"Things change
And friends leave.
And life doesn't stop for anybody."

Stephen Chbosky

Sometimes frightening events occur that are out of our control and coping is difficult. It could be one incident, many incidents over a period of time, or one incident that occurs continuously over the years. Sometimes the trauma is buried in our mind and through the years, something triggers the memory.

But sometimes the trauma is from mistakes that we make. We rationalize our decision at the time, but as time goes by we realize it was a bad decision and we have to deal with the consequences of our actions. Be strong. Pray for strength and keep God a constant in your everyday life.

Mistakes have to be made in order to learn. When my son was very young, he would feel guilty when he made a mistake. I would consistently remind him that making mistakes was normal. It is a necessity, not a luxury, in order to mature. You don't have to be proud of your mistakes and you don't have to tell anybody about them. Wisdom is learning from other people's mistakes and it saves us the pain and suffering from making them ourselves.

“It always seems impossible until it is done.”

Nelson Mandela

As difficult as it sounds, embrace the mistakes, never forget them, learn from them, and notice what a remarkable, humble person you turn out to be. But, don't let the mistake consume your thoughts. Accept it, pray for internal strength and move on.

Sometimes other people judge you on the mistakes you make. Consider the source. Who are they? They are nobody. If they were somebody, they would support you, comfort you and say things to build you back up and help you overcome. I wish I realized this when I was going through guilt ridden times in my life.

"I will not let anyone walk through my mind with their dirty feet" Mahatma Gandhi

Be choosy about who your friends are and no matter how lonely you get, don't settle for someone who is a bad influence. Stay away from people who want to control you and run as fast as you can away from people who make remarks that lower your self esteem. Low self-esteem is much harder to cure than loneliness.

I would rather be lonely than to be with someone who puts me down. Loneliness is easy to cure. Just go to some place where there are people and you will not feel alone. Whether it is a Mall or a park, it is a place where you will definitely lose the feeling of loneliness. I miss the bookstores that used to have coffee and desserts. It was a great place to read, knit, or crochet and have a drink and a snack. You would be surprised to see how many people are there by themselves.

"Time alone builds character.

Don't associate yourself with toxic people.

It's better to be alone and love yourself

than surrounded by people that make you hate yourself."

Robyn Williams

Let God into your heart. Feel His presence.

Love yourself for who you are but continue trying to improve yourself. Realize when someone is giving you constructive criticism or guidance and do not get offended. Appreciate the courage it took for that person to tell you something very difficult. We need good people in our lives, but we need God more.

God is always there to talk to and He is a good listener. You will always find love, compassion and mercy through Him and sometimes, if you listen, He will give you the answer you need. <u>It may not be what you want,</u> but it will be what you *need*. Be patient, it will be worth the wait.

Sometimes we have to hide our feelings towards God because there are people around who put you down for believing. But keeping God a constant in your heart will help you through trying times. Unfortunately, we have managed to love jewelry, cars, money and other materialistic things more than God and His son.

God and His Commandments seem to be fading away. I don't think many ministers, priests or motivational speakers teach it anymore. If they are, no one seems to be listening.

The population is out of control and the world is becoming more chaotic by the minute. So, how do we stay in balance when so much insensitivity and destruction is going on around us?

“Everyone should be quick to listen,

slow to speak

and slow to get angry”

James 1:19

Find someone who shares your interests, morals, values and ethics and keep God as a constant. Pray for those who are suffering. Pray for your own internal strength and become a little hard hearted. Everything in moderation. Realize that no one is perfect and that there will always be differences that can be tolerated. Find out if you prefer religion or if you are more spiritual.

Religion usually means going to church, following certain rituals and doctrines and being part of a group. Sometimes that group is filled with hypocrites and you might find yourself very unhappy.

Whereas spiritual people are individualists who pray, believe in God but not their rituals, and meditate outside the confines of tradition. From what I have read, Jesus was more spiritual and found peace through meditation. David meditated on God's love and wrote beautiful psalms and *kept God constant* in his daily life.

I don't go to church now because I don't feel comfortable, but God is constant in my daily routine. I thank Him everyday for the little things like a hot shower, clean water, convenient food sources, nice clean clothes, and transportation even if it is a very old car. And when my car dies, I will be grateful and thank God for public transportation.

Even though I don't go to church anymore, I miss the times mom and I went to church when I was in high school (1972). Those were good times and helped me overcome my depression.

“Self care is how you take your power back.”

Lalah Dalia

I never told mom I didn't want to live anymore, but I think she sensed that something was very wrong and stepped in to help.

She took me to Christ Church of Georgetown in Washington, DC. on Sundays. I admit that when I walked into that church, I felt a sense of calm and my antagonistic feelings toward mom disappeared. Afterwards, she would take me to Maison de Crepe for lunch. It was also located in Georgetown, DC. Besides being the best food in the world, it was fattening and I think she wanted me to gain weight. Dad started taking me to The Ponderosa one day a week and he ordered liver and onions. He told me it was high in iron and I was anemic. It tasted very good. I really enjoyed the attention and I felt loved by both of them.

Being thankful for the good and the bad moments is vital to good mental health.

When bad things happen, there is a reason. You just don't know it at the time because your mind is consumed with grief. Every time someone causes me grief and heartache, I know God has something wonderful for me just around the corner.

The last thing I want to mention is the concept of forgiveness. Jesus wanted us to understand the importance of it.

The word forgiveness is often misunderstood.

“Forgiveness is not an occasional act;

it is a permanent attitude.”

Martin Luther King, Jr.

Often people say, "if you forgive me you will give me another chance." That has nothing to do with forgiveness. You can forgive someone but not want them back in your life because they are toxic.

The sole purpose of forgiveness is so the injured person can find peace within themself. It is used to erase the hurt and anger. God also said if you forgive those who hurt you, He will forgive you. I think I forgive my brother and sister but if I ever saw them again, I have a bad feeling that hate and anger would overcome my well-being. So, I guess I don't forgive them. I don't know, but I am trying.

Forgiveness has nothing to do with the person who caused the hurt/injury. You do not have to keep them in your life.

I realize there are people who have problems far worse than the ones I mentioned in my book. But, regardless of the specific situations, the concept is the same. All of us share in the feelings of loneliness, neglect, hurt, loss, devastation, betrayal and mind-numbing trauma which requires faith and a strong spirit to see outside of the bubble we are living in. The pain does go away and good times replace the bad *eventually.* There are many solutions to a given problem so if one doesn't work, try another.

Just keep trying. Be tenacious.

"At some point you just have to let go

of what you thought should happen and live

in what is happening."

Heather Hepler

"God is still writing your story,

quit trying to steal the pen.

Trust the author."

Keitumetse Manoto?

Have faith that things will get better;
be tenacious so you don't give up or lose focus;
be patient so you can last the test of time;
have unrelenting loyalty to God and
be determined to solve your problems.

It might sound crazy but I believe that when people are in the habit of being angry all the time that they go through withdrawal when they try to stop.

If necessary, find someone who will help you.

Keep God constant in your daily routine. It works.

Well, that's it for the conclusion of my book. I truly hope it helps.

Warmest wishes,
Mary Louise Sanders

Dear Lord,

Walk before me to clear the way and protect me. Introduce the right people into my life and move the wrong people out of the way. Find it in Your heart to take away my worries and my regrets. Allow me to recharge my soul, renew my hope and fill my heart with joy. Please forgive me for all of my sins.

Amen

"We all need words to live by,
To inspire us and guide us,
Words to give us courage
When the trials of life betide us -
And the words that never fail us
Are the words from God above,
Words of comfort and of courage
Filled with wisdom and with love -"

Helen Steiner Rice

"God has not promised skies always blue,
Flower strewn pathways all of our lives through,
God has not promised sun without rain,
Joy without sorrow, peace without pain.

But God has promised strength for the day,
Rest for the laborer, light on the way,
Grace for the trials, help from above,
Unfailing sympathy, undying love."

Annie Johnson Flint

Made in United States
Orlando, FL
16 June 2024

47940908R00059